MONSTERS

MARTIANS

BY DON NARDO

KIDHAVEN PRESS

An imprint of Thomson Gale, a part of The Thomson Corporation

Detroit • New York • San Francisco • New Haven, Conn. • Waterville, Maine • London

THOMSON

---★--- ™

GALE

For more information, contact
KidHaven Press
27500 Drake Rd.
Farmington Hills, MI 48331-3535
Or you can visit our Internet site at http://www.gale.com

LIBRARY OF CONGRESS CATALOGING-IN-PUBLICATION DATA

Nardo, Don, 1947-
  Martians / by Don Nardo.
    p. cm.—(Monsters)
  Includes bibliographical references and index.
  ISBN 978-0-7377-3639-7 (hardcover)
  1. Martians in mass media—Juvenile literature. 2. Popular culture—Juvenile literature. I. Title.
  P96.M38.N37 2008
  809'.915—dc22

                                                              2007030616

ISBN: 0-7377-3639-9
Printed in the United States of America

CONTENTS

Chapter 1

The Birth of Martians

Many science fiction books and movies have shown people living on the planet Mars. These people are called "Martians." They are usually intelligent creatures and they often want to invade and conquer Earth. With a few exceptions, most movie Martians are monsters or the "bad guys."

Filmgoers have been fascinated by Martians for a long time. Since the late 1930s, a movie about the planet Mars (or just about Martians) has been featured almost every year. In fact, the Martian invasion theme has been so popular that people often use the term *Martians* to describe all **extraterrestrials** (beings from outer space). Phrases such as "the Martians have landed!" have also become familiar in everyday speech.

Martians have been a favorite movie subject for many years.

Early Ideas About Other Planets

Many people believe that it's normal to think of Mars as the home of warlike beings. Mars is the fourth planet from the Sun (after Mercury, Venus, and Earth). It sometimes comes within 35 million miles (56 million km) of Earth. That is quite close in relation to other planets. Mars is one of the brightest objects in the night sky. It also has a reddish, or fiery, color. The ancient Babylonians, Greeks, and Romans all linked the planet Mars with their gods of war. It was also a common belief that when Mars was high in the sky, there was more death and destruction on Earth.

In ancient times, people also thought that there was life on Mars and other planets. They believed that a god (or gods) had created the stars and the planets; so it seemed unthinkable that a god would create a world without life. As the fourth-century B.C. Greek philosopher Metrodorus said, "To consider the Earth as the only populated world in infinite [endless] space is as absurd [crazy] as to assert that in an entire [whole] field of millet, only one grain will grow."[1]

A Growing Belief

Over the centuries, a few educated people held on to the idea of life on other planets. Among them were Italian astronomer Giordano Bruno and German astronomer Johannes Kepler, both born in the 1500s.

These men argued that intelligent creatures lived on other planets. The people of the Catholic Church did not like this idea and they burned Bruno at the stake for supporting it. But the idea didn't go away. In 1776, the famous American writer Thomas Paine (author of the pamphlet *Common Sense*) said: "The inhabitants [people who live] of each of the worlds of which our [solar] system is composed enjoy the same opportunities of knowledge as we do."[2] The French astronomer Camille Flammarion (1842–1925) argued a similar point. He was a strong supporter of the idea that intelligent beings were out there, including Martians.

The Martian Canals

The idea of intelligent Martians became even more popular in 1877. This was partly because of a mistake in a translated document. In that year, Italian astronomer Giovanni Schiaparelli (1835–1910) pointed his large telescope at the planet Mars and saw faint lines crisscrossing the planet's surface. He called these lines *canali*, which means

German astronomer Johannes Kepler believed that there was intelligent life on other planets.

"channels" in Italian. By channels, Schiaparelli meant natural waterways, such as rivers.

However, most newspapers and journals translated *canali* into English as "canals." The term *canal* means an **artificial**, or human-made, waterway. So many people thought the lines on Mars were possible evidence of intelligent creatures living there. The French astronomer Flammarion certainly saw it that way. In his 1892 book *The Planet Mars*, he said:

 Martians

The actual conditions on Mars are such that it would be wrong to deny [say it wasn't true] that it could be inhabited by human species whose intelligence and methods of action could be far superior to [better than] our own. Neither can we deny that they could have straightened the original rivers and

When Giovanni Schiaparelli, through his telescope, saw lines crisscrossing the surface of Mars, many people believed this to be evidence of life on the planet.

built up a system of canals with the idea of producing a planet-wide circulation system.[3]

A wealthy American named Percival Lowell (1855–1916) also believed in the existence of intelligent Martians. In 1894, he built Lowell **Observatory** in Flagstaff, Arizona, so that he could study Mars and the creatures that lived there. He decided that since Mars was a dry world, the Martians had to build canals to carry their small water supplies across large deserts. Lowell wrote three popular books about the red planet: *Mars* (1895), *Mars and Its Canals* (1906), and *Mars as the Abode of Life* (1908).

THE FIRST MARTIAN INVASION

The books written by Lowell, Flammarion, and other astronomers of that time all had one thing in common: they saw Martians staying on the planet Mars. The idea that these creatures could travel through space to Earth was something these scientists were not willing to consider.

But soon a popular fiction writer took the idea one step further. He was the brilliant and talented English novelist H.G. Wells (1866–1946). Wells was interested in the constant talk of intelligent Martians, and in 1898 he published *The War of the Worlds*. Wells begins the book with the idea that Mars is starting to become too dry for creatures to live there. In an effort to survive, the Martians decide to attack and

In 1898 H.G. Wells wrote The War of the Worlds, *a novel about Martians invading Earth.*

take over the wetter, greener Earth. The book opens with the following chilling words:

> No one would have believed in the last years of the nineteenth century that this world was being watched keenly and closely by intelligences greater than man's and yet as mortal [something that dies] as his own. . . . Across the gulf [big area] of space, minds that are to our minds as ours are to those of the beasts that perish, intellects vast and cool and unsympathetic, regarded this Earth with envious eyes, and slowly and surely drew their plans against us.[4]

Wells sees the Martians as slimy, slug-like creatures. They travel about in huge war machines.

The Birth of Martians 11

These advanced weapons move quickly around the countryside on tall mechanical legs and fire deadly heat rays at people and buildings. Many towns and cities are destroyed, and the humans on Earth are in great danger. But then suddenly, the Martians begin to die. They are not used to the germs and diseases on Earth that humans have been able to overcome. "After all man's devices had failed," Wells writes, the invaders were slain "by the humblest things that God, in his wisdom, had put upon this Earth."[5]

SEEMINGLY ENDLESS MARTIANS

The War of the Worlds was very popular and became one of the first classic science fiction books. The novel also inspired a great number of books and short stories about Martians throughout the twentieth century. In many of these stories, the Martians, or other aliens, attack Earth.

However, a few writers used a different approach. Ray Bradbury (b. 1920), for example, did the opposite by making humans the invaders. In his classic work *The Martian Chronicles* (1950), Earth people land on Mars. There, they find an old and peaceful civilization. And thanks to the germs the humans bring with them, that civilization is wiped out. Just as human germs on Earth wipe out the Martians

Opposite: Wells described Martians moving about in long-legged war machines and firing deadly heat rays.

in Wells's book, this time, in *The Martian Chronicles*, humans bring the germs to Mars itself.

Books and stories are not the only forms of entertainment that have featured life on Mars. Around the same time that Wells published *The War of the Worlds,* the first silent films were being made. As time went on, movies became extremely popular and filmmakers soon learned that movies about Martians and Martian invaders would attract large audiences.

CHAPTER 2

MARTIANS IN THE MOVIES

So many movies have been made about Mars and Martians that if we listed them, we would fill many pages. Some films were based on short stories and books, such as H.G. Wells's *War of the Worlds* and Ray Bradbury's *Martian Chronicles*. Other Martian films had original stories and characters. Some were poorly made, with amateur acting and poor special effects. Others were well designed, exciting, and realistic. But most Martian films had one thing in common—they drew large audiences. This is because they encouraged people's fascination about life on the red planet.

Early Martian Movies

Most Martian films featured movement and sound, a technique that began just before 1930. However, a few filmmakers did try to feature Martians in the silent era, which began around the turn of the century. The earliest of all the Martian movies appears to have been *A Trip to Mars*, made in 1910. In this film, a human scientist discovers a special powder. When he sprinkles it on himself he is able to fly and he ends up on Mars. There, he encounters a huge, hideous monster and is almost killed before he manages to escape and return to Earth.

Among the other silent Mars movies were *A Message from Mars* (1913) and *Aelita, Queen of Mars* (1924). *Aelita, Queen of Mars* was made in the Soviet Union (a former country of eastern Europe and northern Asia). In the film, a Soviet scientist discovers life on Mars. When he travels there in a rocket, he tries to help the Martian workers who are being treated badly by an evil **dictator**.

Most of the first sound films about Mars showed wicked individuals ruling over the Martian people. These were mainly low-budget movies based on characters from newspaper comic strips. The most popular movies were those about the adventures of the space-age hero Flash Gordon, played by Buster Crabbe. In *Flash Gordon's Trip to Mars* (1938), Flash discovers a Martian plot to conquer Earth. Azuma, queen of Mars, and Ming the Merciless, the evil

In the 1930s, Flash Gordon movies, which often had a Martian theme, were popular.

emperor of the planet Mongo, had made the plan, but Flash was able to stop the invasion.

THE USE OF ROCKETS

Only a few months after the release of the film *Flash Gordon's Trip to Mars*, World War II started in Europe. During that terrible time, which lasted from 1939 to 1945, very few science fiction films were made. It was not until the late 1940s that film-makers began releasing Martian movies again.

Many of these post-war films took advantage of a recent breakthrough in technology—rocket science. In World War II, the Germans had introduced rockets as weapons. The United States and the Soviet Union continued to research rocket science after the war. People became interested in the possibility of using rockets to carry people into space. And filmmakers took advantage of that interest by making movies about flights to Mars.

The first important film of this kind was *Rocketship XM*, released in 1950. In this movie, four men and a woman are in a rocketship bound for the moon. During the trip, a mechanical failure causes them to stray off-course and they end up on Mars. The explorers then find that the red planet was once home to civilized creatures. But the effects of a nuclear war have led to a society of simple Martian creatures living in caves. The film *Flight to Mars* (1951) also shows humans riding a rocketship to Mars. In this film, the Martians try to steal the visitors' ship so they can fly to Earth and conquer it.

What Would a Martian Look Like?

Some of the early Martian movies showed Martians in the form of humans. And for a long time most filmgoers welcomed this idea. Few people understood that in reality, it was very unlikely that beings from another planet would look exactly like humans.

Opposite top: Some of the early movies showed Martians with human form.

Opposite bottom: Other films showed Martians in ugly and vicious nonhuman forms.

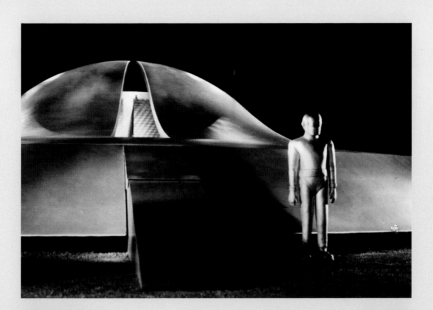

As the Martian movie craze continued, filmmakers began to accept this reality. Several Martian-themed movies of the 1950s and 1960s showed the creatures of the red planet in non-human form. One of the first of these films was *Invaders from Mars* (1953). The movie begins with a little boy waking up in the middle of the night. He watches as a spaceship lands in his backyard and burrows under the ground. The boy soon learns that Martian invaders are kidnapping people and turning them into mindless slaves. The film has two types of Martians. The leader is a bodiless head with tentacles, and its followers are tall, ape-like creatures with huge eyes.

A number of Martian films that followed had even more horrible monsters. In *It, the Terror from Beyond Space* (1958), for example, "It" is a beast with claws and big, sharp teeth. It sneaks into a human spacecraft that has landed on Mars. One by one the humans die terrible deaths until the last survivors manage to kill the creature. In *Angry Red Planet* (1959), another group of Earth explorers land on Mars. They fight with various monsters. These include a giant, slimy one-celled Martian and a strange creature that looks like a cross between a bat, a rat, and a spider.

Martian Motives

Over time, movie Martians fell into two main types. The first were creatures like those in *Rocketship XM*,

Angry Red Planet, and *It.* They were simple, ugly, and vicious creatures. Their **motives** were fairly simple—to protect themselves from human invaders or to use humans as a source of food.

The second group of Martian monsters had more complicated motives. These creatures, like those in *Invaders from Mars*, had the technology they needed to travel through space. They wanted to conquer or destroy Earth. The most famous of these were the Martians in producer George Pal's 1953 epic, *The War of the Worlds*. This film was the first attempt to film H.G. Wells's classic novel. Pal shows the invaders causing widespread damage and escaping harm from human weapons, even atomic bombs. Just like the book, the Martians die when they become infected by earthly germs.

HUMANS AT RISK

Many film Martians try to kidnap humans. This happens often because the Martians can no longer reproduce themselves. In *Mars Needs Women* (1966), for example, Martian men try to steal and mate with Earth women. The situation is reversed in *Devil Girl from Mars* (1954). This time Martian women are looking for human men. These examples are low-budget movies, with poor dialogue and cheap special effects. Even more extreme is the kidnapping of Santa Claus by Martians in *Santa Claus Conquers the Martians* (1964) because the Martians wanted to make Earth children less cheerful.

Many critics have called this one of the worst movies ever made.

Bigger Budgets Pay Off

Years later, some Martian movies and television programs were made with bigger budgets and became much more memorable. Among them was a 1979 television mini-series based on Bradbury's *Martian Chronicles*. Even better were some wonderful remakes of earlier Martian films—*Invaders from Mars* in 1986 and famed director Steven Spielberg's *War of the Worlds* in 2005. Other recent big-budget Martian films included *Mars Attacks!* (1996), *Red Planet* (2000), and *Mission to Mars* (2000).

Martians tried to destroy the world in the first movie version of The War of the Worlds.

As Martian movies became more popular, budgets were increased, allowing more advanced special effects.

One important factor links all of these films. The large budgets meant that advanced special effects could be used. Over the past century, the ways in which filmmakers have brought Martians to life have changed considerably.

Chapter 3

Martians Come to Life on Screen

The makers of films about Mars have always faced a difficult challenge. They have had to find ways to make their fictional Martians appear realistic and believable on movie screens. Unfortunately, many movie Martians are not very believable because of a lack of money. Most films about Mars and Martians have had very low budgets. This meant that it was not possible to use advanced special effects.

In fact, during the first six decades of the twentieth century, most science fiction films were

"B" movies. These were small-scale, low-budget films designed for very few people. At the time, most people thought that space travel was impossible. Many filmgoers felt that movies about outer space and aliens were silly and they avoided them. However, a few people found the films inspiring. They were a small, but reliable audience for "B" movies about spaceships and Martians.

Changing Times

In the 1970s, the situation changed dramatically. The United States put men on the moon in 1969, and people began to see space travel and aliens as both possible and interesting. As a result, film studios and producers started to put more money toward science fiction films. Blockbusters such as *Star Wars* (1977), *Close Encounters of the Third Kind* (1977), and *E.T. the Extra-Terrestrial* (1982) made a lot of money at

When the U.S. put the first man on the moon in 1969, moviegoers became more interested in films about space travel and aliens.

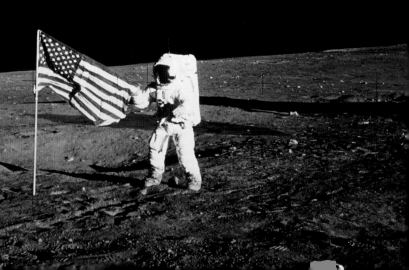

the box office. These films were popular partly because they featured very good special effects. The movies led the way for more big-budget blockbusters about space travel and aliens, including several about Martians.

Realistic Effects

This development in science fiction films caused audiences to change their expectations. Today, film-goers expect a certain amount of realism, such as believable examples of the conditions on other planets, such as Mars.

Space probes have orbited and landed on Mars in recent years. They have shown us the harsh environment of the planet, which has a very thin atmosphere and a lack of surface water. Scientists think there may have been more air and water in the past, but any Martian life that could develop there would not look like human beings. Modern filmmakers are expected to think about these conditions when they make their fictional Martians. Today, audiences would laugh at a film showing Martians as ordinary humans, as they are in the movie *Flash Gordon's Trip to Mars.*

Martians in Human Form

Before humans began to explore space, movie audiences knew nothing about the conditions on Mars. Many people thought that the planet had air and water. And at the time, the idea that creatures

We now know that the harsh environment on Mars could not have produced human-like inhabitants.

on other planets looked like humans was very believable. Most filmgoers accepted human-like creatures living on Mars. And this made it cheap and easy for filmmakers to hire actors and put them in suitable costumes.

Even when these films showed non-human Martians, the simplest, cheapest method was to place an actor in a monster suit. Because the actor had a head, a torso, two arms and two legs, the Martian he played would have the same features. This limited the movie Martians to a human-like form.

Another problem was that most of the monster suits were not very well-made. The suit used in *It, the Terror from Beyond Space*, for example, did not look or move like real skin and muscles. In a couple of scenes, the suit's zipper is also briefly visible. The ape-like Martians in the 1953 version of *Invaders from Mars* are also actors dressed in poor-quality suits.

Mechanical Martians

Some filmmakers of that time tried to avoid showing Martians as human-like creatures. To create more imaginative life forms they tried to use various **mechanical special effects**. The rat-bat-spider in *Angry Red Planet*, for example, was a mechanical puppet. This multi-legged monster looked frightening enough. However, off-camera people used strings, wires, and thin wooden dowels to move it, and its movements were not very lifelike.

Much more realistic mechanical effects were used in the 1953 version of *The War of the Worlds*. This was one of the few science fiction movies of its time with a good budget. The film did well at the box office and went on to win the Academy Award for Best Special Effects.

New Effects

The movie's producer, George Pal, had started out as a special effects expert. So he knew what could and could not be done with the technology available at the time. In H.G. Wells's novel, the Martians ride inside metal boxes supported by tall jointed legs. Pal recognized that making these war machines walk in a realistic way would be too difficult. So he decided to place his Martians inside sleek, manta-ray-shaped flying machines.

Each war machine was a copper model more than 3 feet (1m) across. Copper was chosen because it has an orange-red tinge, reflecting the redness so often linked with Mars. The machines were suspended from thin wires which made the models move, but also carried the electricity that powered the onboard lights and death-rays.

The machines' pilots are only shown in a few scenes of the movie. In one of these scenes, a Martian comes up to a man and a woman in a darkened cellar. The alien-looking creature has a bulky, brown, headless **torso** with one large eye in the middle. The eye has three lenses—one blue, one green, and one red. The Martian also has two tentacle-like arms, each with a three-fingered hand at the end. This unique creature was a large puppet mechanically operated by people off-screen. It was very frightening, especially when it gave out an eerie screech. To create this sound, technicians recorded a woman screaming and played it backwards.

COMPUTER MAGIC

Mechanically-operated devices continued to be used in movies about Mars, but they were soon overtaken by new special effects that produced more realistic results. Computer Generated Imagery (**CGI**) is the main technique used today. It creates lifelike images of make-believe objects or living things on a computer screen. These images are then **animated** so that they move in a realistic way.

The aliens in Mars Attacks! *were created using computer animation.*

For example, the bug-eyed Martians in Tim Burton's *Mars Attacks!* were created using computer animation. The process began with a series of drawings showing the basic design of one of these creatures. Computer animators created a three-dimensional version of the Martian on a computer screen. Advanced software programs were then used to make the Martian walk and perform other movements. Finally, the computer combined the Martian images with real footage to make them become part of the film itself.

The walking war machines and Martians in Steven Spielberg's version of *The War of the Worlds* also used CGI. Any Martians or other extraterrestrials that humans can imagine can now be brought to life on the screen in a very believable way.

Martians

Chapter 4

Martians in Popular Culture

At the same time Martians were becoming familiar movie monsters, they were also spreading to other areas of popular culture. Thousands of novels and short stories about Martians were written in the twentieth century. Several of these, including H.G. Wells's *The War of the Worlds* and Ray Bradbury's *The Martian Chronicles*, became classics read by people around the world. There were also famous radio and television programs that featured Martians who had traveled to Earth. Some of these visitors were clearly evil and

*Many products, including comic books, followed
the movies' successful Martian themes.*

dangerous. Others were good and even funny.
Many other products also used Martian themes or
images. These included comic books, toys, video
games, lunchboxes, coloring books, and Halloween
costumes.

Classic Novels About Mars

Many different types of Martians have been used in popular culture. But the invaders from Wells's *The War of the Worlds* have been the most popular and are often copied. The classic novel, with its towering Martian war machines destroying Earth, has inspired three major motion pictures. Other products have included a radio show, comic books, poster art, music, and toys all based on the story.

Wells and Bradbury were not the only writers who explored Martian characters and themes. Among the most famous and loved characters of all were those invented by American author

Edgar Rice Burroughs, famous for creating Tarzan, also wrote a series of novels about Mars.

Edgar Rice Burroughs (1875–1950). Today, he is perhaps best known as the creator of the jungle hero Tarzan. But Rice Burroughs is nearly as famous for his series of novels about Mars. In these stories, he gives the red planet an alternate name– Barsoom. The tales follow the exciting adventures of a human named John Carter, who once fought in the American Civil War.

Adventures on Barsoom

In the first book, *A Princess of Mars* (1911–1912), Carter travels to Barsoom. There, he finds that the planet is rapidly drying up. Its huge oceans have almost disappeared and many of its cities are empty. Carter also finds that the people of Barsoom are fighting each other in two groups. A group of human-like creatures versus a group of monstrous creatures with four arms and big tusks.

A Princess of Mars was very popular and many books followed. These included *The Gods of Mars* (1913), *Thuvia, Maid of Mars* (1916), *The Master Mind of Mars* (1927), and *A Fighting Man of Mars* (1930). John Carter also appeared in other areas of popular culture, including a newspaper comic strip in the 1940s, a series of Dell comic books in the 1950s, and several Marvel comic books in the 1970s. A big-budget movie version of Carter's adventures is also scheduled for release in 2008.

Another classic novel about Martians also features a human who goes to Mars and lives with the creatures there. This book is called *Stranger in a Strange Land* (1961) and its author, Robert A. Heinlein, was one of the twentieth century's leading science fiction writers. In the story, young Valentine Michael Smith is the only survivor of the first human expedition to Mars. He is brought up by Martians, and eventually allowed to return to Earth. There, he reveals that he has special mental powers. Smith starts a new religious movement that promises to teach its members to use the powers of their own minds. However, other Earth people see Smith as a dangerous monster and they murder him. *Stranger in a Strange Land* was so popular that it became the first science fiction book to make it onto the *New York Times* best-seller list.

MARTIANS ON THE RADIO

Although many people enjoyed reading novels about Martians, millions of people were terrified by a radio broadcast about them in 1938. A talented young actor named Orson Welles (no relation to H.G. Wells) had recently started a popular radio program. Each week his acting company, the Mercury Theater, presented a fictional drama. To help celebrate Halloween, Welles decided to recreate the plot of H.G. Wells's classic novel; on October 30, the Mercury Theater did its version of *The War of the Worlds.*

Welles's broadcast was different from the original novel in two ways. First, he updated the setting

In 1938 actor Orson Welles broadcast The War of the Worlds *over the radio.*

from London in the 1890s to New Jersey in the 1930s. More importantly, he told much of the story through a series of news bulletins. This approach was meant to be creative, but a number of listeners misunderstood. They thought the news flashes were real and that Earth was actually under attack by invading Martians. Some of them panicked and several even fled their homes.

This unexpected event made real news headlines around the world. In November 1938 alone, an estimated 12,500 newspaper articles were written about the event, and it is still a feature of popular culture today. Each year on Halloween, a Los Angeles radio station, KNX (1070 AM), replays a recording of it. The broadcast was also dramatized in the 1975 ABC television drama *The Night that Panicked America.*

Millions of people all over the world were terrified by Welles's broadcast.

TV Martians

Another Martian arrival on Earth was shown in the popular television series *My Favorite Martian*. The CBS comedy's 107 episodes ran from 1963–1966. Famous stage and screen actor Ray Walston starred as a Martian named Exigius Twelve and a Half (or Exigius for short), whose spacecraft crashed in Los Angeles. He became friends with a human played by Bill Bixby, and they decided to keep Exigius's true identity a secret by giving him the name Uncle Martin. As the series developed, many funny situations took place in which Uncle Martin used some of his advanced powers. These included becoming invisible, reading minds, and communicating with animals.

My Favorite Martian was very popular and is still being repeated on television today. Its popularity led to many other products, including an animated series—*My Favorite Martians*—in the 1970s, and a big-budget movie version in theaters in 1999. This film starred Christopher Lloyd as Uncle Martin and Jeff Daniels as his human pal. Then in 2000, a television commercial for AT&T featured Ray Walston as Uncle Martin, asking how much AT&T would charge for calls to Martians living on Earth. Gold Key Comics also marketed a series of *My Favorite Martian* comic books.

Opposite: My Favorite Martian, *starring Ray Walston, was a favorite TV show in the mid-1960s.*

Glossary

animated: Brought to life. Animation is a technique that brings drawings to life on screen.

artificial: Manufactured or created by people or other intelligent beings.

CGI: Computer Generated Imagery; the use of computers to create special effects for movies and television shows.

dictator: A ruler who forces his or her will on a country and its people.

extraterrestrials: Beings from beyond Earth, usually another planet.

mechanical special effects: In movies and television, making objects move by mechanical means, such as wires, levers, wheels, or remote control signals.

motives: Aims or goals.

Observatory: A room or building used to observe the planets and other features of outer space.

torso: The central part of the body, including the chest and abdomen.

FOR FURTHER EXPLORATION

BOOKS

Jack Cohen and Ian Stewart, *What Does a Martian Look Like: The Science of Extraterrestrial Life*. Hoboken, NJ: Wiley, 2002. A fascinating exploration of what alien beings might look like.

Ken Croswell, *Magnificent Mars*. New York: Free Press, 2003. One of the best recent books about Mars and ongoing human exploration of that planet, including a number of spectacular photos.

William K. Hartman, *A Traveler's Guide to Mars*. New York: Workman, 2003. Discusses the possibilities of humans traveling to Mars, Martian life, and other aspects of the famous "red planet."

Kathleen Krull, *The Night the Martians Landed: Just the Facts*. New York: HarperCollins, 2003. This very well-illustrated and entertaining volume tells the story of the famous 1938 "War of the Worlds" radio broadcast by Orson Welles and the Mercury Theater.

Don Nardo, *The Search for Extraterrestrial Life*. San Diego: Lucent Books, 2006. A detailed exploration of the subject, including sections on potential intelligent aliens and the intriguing possibility that life on Earth may have come from Mars.

H.G. Wells, *The War of the Worlds.* New York: Modern Library, 2002. This is only one of hundreds of available reprints of Wells's classic 1898 science fiction novel that established the idea of Martian invaders.

WEB SITES

About Hollywood Movies, "Behind the Scenes of *War of the Worlds.***"** (http://movies.about.com/od/waroftheworlds/a/warworld022305.htm.) An in-depth discussion of the making of Steven Spielberg's recent remake of the 1953 version of H.G. Wells's classic book about Martians invading Earth.

Orson Welles and Mercury Theater, "The War of the Worlds by H.G. Wells." (http://members.aol.com/jeff1070/script.html.) The actual script of Orson Welles's famous 1938 radio broadcast that made thousands of people believe that Earth was being invaded by Martians.

Paul Brian, "Study Guide for Ray Bradbury's *The Martian Chronicles.***"** (http://members.aol.com/jeff1070/script.html.) An excellent general overview of the plot and themes of Bradbury's famous book about intelligent Martians.

Planetary Society, "The Search for Extraterrestrial Intelligence: A Short History." (http://www.planetary.org/html/UPDATES/seti/history/History00.htm.) A very informative overview of the longstanding efforts to find intelligent life on other worlds, including Mars.

MOVIES TO RENT

Five Million Years to Earth (1967)
Strange beings inside an ancient Martian spaceship dis-
covered beneath London's subway system stir to life,
causing widespread chaos in this classic film.

Invaders from Mars (1953)
The original version of a story filmed again in the 1980s
under the same title. A young boy witnesses the landing of a Martian spaceship and becomes involved in
the fight against the invaders.

Mars Attacks (1996)
Filmmaker Tim Burton's humorous tribute to alien
invasion movies is well-filmed and entertaining, and
has a star-studded cast.

Red Planet (2000)
Val Kilmer stars in this spectacular film about human
astronauts landing on Mars and finding Martian life.

War of the Worlds (1953)
The first film version of H.G. Wells's great book about
invading Martians won the Oscar for best special
effects, which included green death rays that evapo-
rate both people and buildings.

War of the Worlds (2005)
Steven Spielberg directed this large-scale remake of
the 1953 version of Wells's book. In this movie, the
Martians do not land; rather, they burrow upward
from the ground, having landed in prehistoric times.

INDEX

PICTURE CREDITS

ABOUT THE AUTHOR

In addition to his acclaimed volumes on ancient civilizations, historian and award-winning writer Don Nardo has written or edited many books about strange phenomena, including famous monsters. These include volumes on the mythical snake-headed Medusa, the legendary one-eyed Cyclops, robots running wild in literature and movies, the possible existence of extraterrestrial life, and numerous books about the non-human creatures of ancient Egyptian, Greek, Roman, Persian, and Nordic mythology. Mr. Nardo lives with his wife Christine in Massachusetts.